Britain's Andy Murray leaves the stage of his greatest triumph, clutching the men's singles trophy on Centre Court at Wimbledon

CONTENTS

A Mirror publication
Head of Syndication & Licensing: Fergus McKenna
Mirrorpix: David Scripps
020 7293 3858

Produced by Trinity Mirror Sport Media
PO BOX 48, Liverpool, L69 3EB
ISBN 9781907324284

Managing Director: Ken Rogers
Senior Editor: Steve Hanrahan
Senior Art Editor: Rick Cooke
Editor: Paul Dove
Compiled and written by: Alan Jewell,
Chris McLoughlin, Chris Brereton
Designed by: Lee Ashun, Colin Sumpter,
Alison Barkley, Jamie Dunmore
Sub-edited by: Adam Oldfield,
James Cleary, Jim Connor

Part of the Mirror Collection
© Published by Trinity Mirror 2013
Images: Mirrorpix, PA Photos, Trinity Mirror
Printed by Wyndeham Group

HOW ANDY FINALLY BROUGHT BRITISH TENNIS HOME

by **Oliver Holt**, Daily Mirror

> **A little before 7pm, a little girl in a floral print dress ended her day at the All England Club by making a pilgrimage.**

Her parents ushered her forward so they could take her picture and she stood on tiptoes and reached up to hold the cold hand of an old hero.

The bronze statue of Fred Perry gazed down at her from its place in the shadows outside Centre Court until she moved on and allowed another to take her place.

Maybe fewer people will visit next year. Or maybe they will come in the same numbers, just in a different spirit. Because July 7, 2013, was a day when British sport finally let go of a great slab of its past. A day when Andy Murray's stunning straight sets demolition of Novak Djokovic allowed the ghosts of Wimbledon failure to float away into the clear blue sky.

This was a personal triumph for Murray, of course, a second Grand Slam title to go with last year's US Open glory.

It was a triumph that suggests he could now go on to become the world number one, win more Slams and write his name large in tennis history.

But there were times in the aftermath of his win when it was easy to become lost in the wider significance of the moment. Because when Murray brought closure to the 77-year quest to become the first Briton since Perry to win the Wimbledon men's singles title, it was time for farewells.

Farewell to those agonised cries of 'C'mon Tim' that were the shrill accompaniment to Tim Henman's quartet of near misses. Farewell to the doomed annual lionisation of also-rans like Jeremy Bates, Buster Mottram and John Lloyd.

Farewell to the memories of Roger Taylor's three semi-final defeats in the late 60s and early 70s and Mike Sangster's in 1961. Farewell to the sensation of hearing the name of Perry, who won the men's title three times between 1934 and 1936, and feeling its stinging reproach.

And, best of all, farewell to the idea that British tennis is for losers and spoiled little rich kids.

At 5.24pm, after three hours and nine minutes of relentless combat under a cruel sun, Murray bade farewell to all that.

In his moment of victory, he turned to the press box with an expression of unfettered joy. And in return, many of the lucky few packed into Centre Court wept unashamedly in relief and exultation.

Let's be blunt about it: most tennis fans had begun to believe they would never see a British winner of Wimbledon in their lifetime.

The quest felt as if it had become cursed, like the Boston Red Sox pursuit of the World Series once did and like the Chicago Cubs' chase still does.

Watching from the Royal Box, how Wayne Rooney must have envied Murray's overwhelming sense of release from the crushing burden of expectation.

The two quasi-religious quests for British sport have been a men's winner of Wimbledon and the England football team winning the World Cup. Murray just fixed the first. The second seems as far away as ever.

What a way to fix it, too. What a magnificent, dominant, confident crushing victory over the world number one.

After the sporting wonders of 2012, suddenly Murray, the British and Irish Lions and the England cricket team are suggesting 2013 might not be an anti-climax after all.

It was so hot when Murray and Djokovic walked out into the arena that Centre Court looked like a scene from a period drama as supporters tried to cool themselves with fans.

It must have felt like walking into hell but Murray did not flinch. He began as if he was executing a slow exorcism of the demons of British tennis.

The first rally seemed to last an eternity as these two men, who have contested three of the last four Grand Slam finals, battered the ball at each other from the baseline.

Djokovic blinked first, hitting a forehand long and had to save three break points before he won the game.

Murray had another series of break points in Djokovic's second service game and when he took one at the fourth attempt, it was greeted with a massive cheer. It was the first hint of what was to come. Murray burned with a refusal to give up on anything, however hopeless the cause.

If Djokovic looked restless and troubled, perhaps affected by his marathon semi-final victory over Juan Martin Del Potro, Murray seethed with energy. Never give up, never give up, his tennis shouted out.

At 2-2 and 40-0 down, he still managed to chase down a ➤

shot from Djokovic that seemed like a lost cause. Even when he got it back over the net, it looked as if it would be an easy kill. But Djokovic took his eye off it and put his volley into the net. That was the match in microcosm.

In those first few games, Murray and Djokovic threw everything at each other in the inferno.

The first five games took nearly half an hour but when the score reached 3-3, Murray broke Djokovic's serve to love.

Another huge explosion of joy rolled around Centre Court when he held his serve to love.

The tennis was balletic, full of scything slices and extravagant forehand sweeps, stationary hitting and fast dashes for drop shots.

Murray found himself 4-2 down in the second set but broke back when Djokovic served a double fault.

Djokovic started to fret, making unsuccessful line call challenges and complaining bitterly to the umpire. The crowd gave him the slow hand-clap. Murray broke his serve to lead 6-5 and served out to take the second set.

History was tantalisingly close now. Djokovic's game wasn't working. He tried to shorten points with drop shots and Murray chased them down relentlessly. When he broke to lead 5-4 in the third set, the tension was almost unbearable.

After 77 years, it was down to one game.

What a game it was, too. If the 1980 Wimbledon men's final gave us The Tie-Break this was The Game.

It lasted for 12 minutes of nerve-shredding drama.

Murray raced into a 40-0 lead then squandered all three Championship points.

Djokovic held several break points – one volley teetered on top of the net before falling apologetically on to Murray's side – but the Scot saved them.

Eventually, when dark thoughts were turning to the damage done to Murray's psyche if Djokovic escaped now, Murray summoned one final effort. Djokovic hit the ball into the net and it was over.

Since Perry won the men's title, 18 players from the USA, one from France, nine from Australia, one from Egypt, two from Spain, one from Czechoslovakia, two from Sweden, two from Germany, one from Holland, one from Croatia, one from Switzerland and one from Serbia have won it, too.

Now there's one from Britain to add to the list.

At the post-match press conference, a veteran US commentator called Bud Collins, a little frail now and in his 80s, spoke to Murray from the floor and told him he had known Perry.

"Every year I'd come to Wimbledon," he said, "and I'd say to Fred 'is this the year?' He'd say 'I don't think so'.

"It went on like that for several years and finally Fred couldn't make it any more. Anyway, he kept hoping this day would happen and I'm glad to report that it has."

Murray listened with a smile and thanked him. Out by Centre Court, as night fell, Perry's statue began to disappear in the darkness.

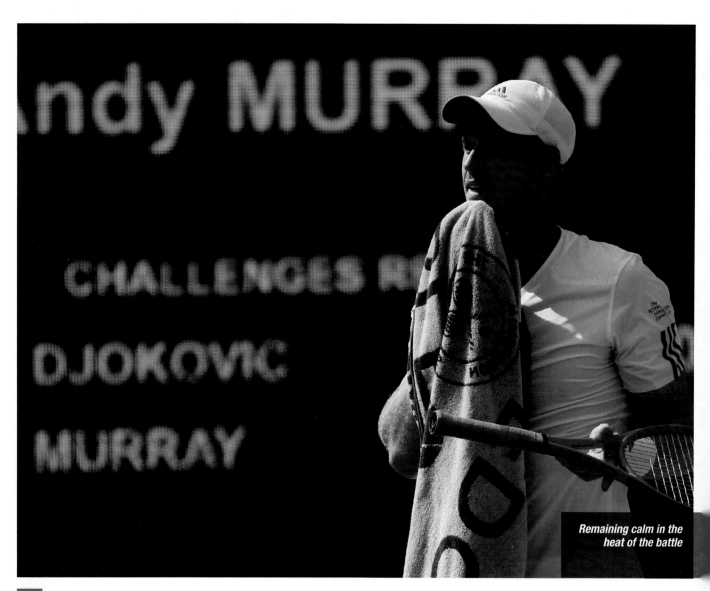

Remaining calm in the heat of the battle

WHY WE SHOULD SALUTE ANDY MURRAY FOR WRINGING EVERY LAST DROP OF ACHIEVEMENT FROM HIS TALENT

by **Andy Dunn**, Sunday Mirror

Sporting history would be a dreary, desolate wasteland without the flawed genius.

We're still painfully aware of Paul Gascoigne, not for his talent, but the fact that so much of his life has been undermined by familiar human frailties.

For being a bit of a rum lad and putting the Australians to the sword in one series, we lionise Andrew Flintoff, forgetting a career Test batting average of 31.77 and bowling average of 32.78 were meagre returns on his talent.

We romanticise James Hunt, not solely for his 10 Grand Prix victories and World Championship success of 1976, but for the partying regime that accompanied them.

Ricky Hatton's post-fight binges might not have been as celebrated as his brave ring triumphs, but they were part of what made him a hero of the common man.

And let's not even start on George Best.

The 'where did it all go wrong' legend has become a touchstone for those who love their heroes seduced by demons. And there is nothing wrong with that.

There is something impossibly romantic about a dreamily talented individual succumbing to destructive temptation.

Now we should salute a different genre of idol. One who wrings every last drop of achievement from his talent.

This is not to undervalue the wealth of Andy Murray's natural ability. He is blessed with an extraordinary gift. But here is a sportsman possessed by the desire to ensure not one shred of that ability goes untapped.

Just under a year ago – in that Olympic summer – tales of sacrifice and determination proliferated. But to maintain an obsessive level of commitment over a lengthy, successful, lucrative professional career needs special character.

The comfort zone is a deeply alluring place for an athlete already feted and already with millions in the bank. Murray has never been tempted. But then we should not be surprised.

While the extravagant funding towards developing British tennis players is intended to nurture champions of the future, it doubles as a comfort zone.

➤ Murray never sought such a cosseted career launch. From mid-Scotland, he travelled hundreds of miles to play in boys' tournaments. As a teenager, he took himself to the academy in Barcelona. Murray's single-mindedness seems everlasting. In terms of titles, he has been a junior member of a glorious gang of four.

It would be easy to settle for that. Yet there will never be any settling.

Just as his game often appears to be based on remorseless pursuit, so does his career. But it seems not to be a pursuit of material trappings or unanimous public acclaim. It is a pursuit of maximising his gift.

In an interview two years ago, prior to the 2012 Grand Slam breakthrough, Murray said this: "… if you are prepared to sacrifice just a little more than your opponent, it will give you an advantage. If you've done the extra mile, you might have the better of him.

"I'd love everyone to see the work that goes into it, because this is not just a case of having talent and believing that is all it takes. I am trying so hard to get that edge."

That hard work paid off in New York last year and it paid off on Centre Court today. If it hadn't, Murray would simply have redoubled his effort to find that edge.

Glamorous? No.

Chronicles of sport will always be sprinkled with the stardust of the flamboyant, the extravagant, the tortured and the troubled.

But there should always be a place for those who are unrelenting in their quest to make the most out of what life has granted them.

And I doubt there has been a British sportsman or woman as unrelenting as Andy Murray.

IN HIS OWN WORDS

"Winning Wimbledon is the pinnacle of tennis, the last game almost increased that feeling. It pretty much took everything out of me."

"I worked so hard in that last game. They will be the hardest few points I have to play in my life. Some of the shots Novak came up with were unbelievable."

"I won the first three points and then it was mentally the hardest game ever. I didn't feel great after it went from 40-0 to deuce. I started feeling nervous and thinking of what just happened. Very rarely will you get broken on grass from 40-0 up when serving."

"I can't even really remember what happened, my mind was everywhere. At the end, I didn't really know what was going on."

"I have played in a lot of Slam finals, all against Roger or Novak. Roger is probably the greatest player ever, Novak is one of the mentally strongest ever. I never had experience on my side, to beat him was so tough, it was such a tough match."

"It was so hot as well. I hadn't played any matches in the heat of the day. Since the clay-court season, since I missed the French Open with my back, it had been cool. I hadn't played at all in those sort of conditions. The first few games were brutal as well. It was 30 minutes for the first four games."

"I only slept for an hour and a half [after winning Wimbledon] so I was pretty beat up when I woke up. But it's a beautiful day to wake up as Wimbledon champion."

"For the last four or five years it's been very tough, very stressful, a lot of pressure. The last two days were not easy because it's just everywhere you go."

"It's so hard to avoid everything because of how big this event is, but also because of the history and no Brit having won for so long. It's been very, very difficult."

"I hope that it won't be another 77 years before another Brit wins it again, but it is not an easy tournament to win."

"Winning Wimbledon...I can't get my head around that. I still can't believe it's happened."

THE FINAL

Andy Murray shattered the biggest hoodoo in British sport and Novak Djokovic, the fiercest competitor in tennis, as he won his first Wimbledon championship in glorious fashion. *Here's how he did it...*

FIRST SET:

Under a brutal, burning sun, Djokovic served first and Murray made life uncomfortable for the Serb from the start, winning an 18-shot rally on the first point that set the tone for what was to come. The Brit earned three break points but Djokovic saw them off thanks to three first serves.

After a regulation Murray hold, the Brit got stuck into the 2011 champion again, attacking from the baseline with thunderous intent. Djokovic looked nervous as he was making uncharacteristic errors and Murray created more break points. The Serb saved three but on the fourth, Murray dispatched a forehand to strike the first blow.

Djokovic donned a cap at the changeover, narrowed his gaze and roared straight back, forcing errors from Murray with the ferocity and accuracy of his hitting, earning three break points of his own. When the home hope put a forehand into the net, we were back on serve at 2-2.

TURNING POINT:

After a hold apiece, the so-often crucial seventh game of the set proved decisive. Murray's groundstrokes scorched the turf and proved too hot for Djokovic too handle as he broke the Serb to love. The Brit and his supporters roared their approval. At this stage Djokovic had already made 13 unforced errors. Earlier in the tournament he played two whole sets without making a single one. Both men were pushing each other to the limit but Murray was maintaining greater control, moving brilliantly and tracking down balls before returning them with interest. He was also winning more points on his first serve than Djokovic – Murray was reading the Serb's delivery and getting the vast majority of them back in play.

It was a very nervous start to the eighth game from Murray as he served successive double faults to leave himself on the back foot at 0-30. Two points later it was 15-40 and Djokovic had an opportunity to restore parity at the business end of the set. An ace and volley put-away took it to deuce. Another volley behind a heavy forehand sealed the hold and Murray was a game away from the first set.

Djokovic held to force Murray to serve it out and the Brit did so in style – two aces and another unreturnable serve ensured Djokovic wouldn't get a sniff. It was a hold to love and, just like the 2012 final, Murray had the first set on the board, 6-4, with an hour gone. Could he capitalise this time?

FIRST SET STATS:

Aces: Murray 5, Djokovic 1
Double faults: Murray 2, Djokovic 1
1st serves in: Murray 63%, Djokovic 60%
1st serve points won: Murray 84%, Djokovic 54%
Break points won: Murray 2/8, Djokovic 1/5
Winners: Murray 17, Djokovic 6
Unforced errors: Murray 6, Djokovic 17

SECOND SET:

Both men held their opening service games – the pace remained unrelenting as the greatest defenders in the sport fought to pierce their opponent's armour. Murray was still getting the better of the baseline exchanges and Djokovic was coming to the net far more than normal, seeking to shorten the points. He was well out of his comfort zone but held for 2-1.

In the next Murray service game, the Serb struck. Djokovic's power and angles took Murray out of position and a netted forehand following another awe-inspiring 30-stroke rally gave Djokovic the first break of the second set at 3-1.

The previously raucous crowd were quietened for the first time in the match but Murray soon had them roaring their approval with a backhand winner that gave him a slight opening at 15-30. However, a forehand volley and big first serve quickly took it away as Djokovic backed up the break to lead 4-1.

Murray now also put a cap on to protect himself from the glare of the sun and stayed in the set with a straightforward hold. When these men meet their matches almost always ebb and flow and this one was no different. At 4-2, Murray was all over Djokovic again, as he fought to halt the momentum behind the Serb. A tremendous forehand earned two break-back points but both opportunities passed by as he missed with a forehand and backhand. Djokovic wasn't out of trouble, though. A stunning backhand return and flat forehand brought up another break point and when Djokovic double-faulted, we were back on serve at 4-3.

The Briton had to dig deep again in his next service game as an overhead gave Djokovic another break point. It was saved by an ace that just clipped the outside edge of the line as Djokovic appealed in vain to Hawk-Eye. After Murray earned a game point, Djokovic took him back to deuce again before a cute drop-shot closed out a meaty hold as he clawed himself back to 4-4.

Djokovic held comfortably for 5-4 and Murray had to serve to stay in the set. Although he was off target with a couple of shots, he was able to eke out the game and take it to 5-5.

TURNING POINT:

As Djokovic faltered in the eleventh game of the set, so Murray, unwavering and intently focused, seized his opportunity. The Serb couldn't handle a backhand from his opponent and volleyed into the net. Then he lost his composure as he believed a Murray shot had gone long, but couldn't stop play as he was out of challenges. He vented his frustration at the umpire to no avail, but Hawk-Eye showed the ball clipped the line anyway. After a netted forehand from the rattled Djokovic, Murray had two break points. The first was saved with an overhead but another jerky forehand found the net and Murray had a crucial, crucial break. He would serve for a two-set lead.

As when he served for the first set, Murray took care of business with the minimum of fuss. Booming first serves, including an ace at 40-0, gave him a two-set lead. Roars rang out all around the grounds and his support team were on their feet. He was a set away from the holiest of holy grails, but he was facing a man in Djokovic who just doesn't know when he is beaten. There was still plenty of work to be done, but Britain believed. Most importantly, so did Murray.

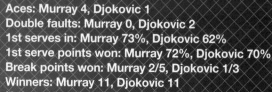

SECOND SET STATS:

Aces: Murray 4, Djokovic 1
Double faults: Murray 0, Djokovic 2
1st serves in: Murray 73%, Djokovic 62%
1st serve points won: Murray 72%, Djokovic 70%
Break points won: Murray 2/5, Djokovic 1/3
Winners: Murray 11, Djokovic 11
Unforced errors: Murray 5, Djokovic 12

The frustration shows as Djokovic struggles to contain an inspired Murray

THIRD SET:

Murray sensed the opportunity to go in for the kill and didn't allow his intensity to drop at the start of the third. He had Djokovic at 0-30 and although the Serb brought it back to 30-30, a fierce forehand eked out another break point. Murray stopped play in the next rally as he thought Djokovic had gone long and his instinct proved correct as Hawk-Eye showed it was out. An immediate break for the Briton and expectation rose even further.

Murray's next service game passed by in a flash as he held for 2-0. After yet more errors from the Serb, it was 0-30 on the Djokovic serve and the match was in danger of running away from him. However, the world number one showed the nerve and skill that has brought him six Grand Slam titles to win four points in a row and get on the board in the third set.

Serving at 2-1, Murray again stopped play in the middle of the rally as he thought a Djokovic shot had landed long but this time his judgement was faulty. After going long himself, he was in a hole at 0-30. Although two big serves brought it back to 30-30, Djokovic went cross-court for a break point and when Murray put a volley wide, the crowd gasped and it was level again at 2-2.

The Serb, on the back foot for so much of the afternoon, was now the aggressor and held easily before again piling the pressure on Murray, who was suddenly missing the target with his groundstrokes. At 15-40 he sent a forehand into the net and Djokovic had won four games in a row.

Was the third set gone? Not a bit of it. He fired a forehand straight at the Serb to bring up 0-30, before a backhand winner took us to 15-40 and two break-back points. The first was saved with a big serve but Djokovic couldn't do anything about the second. We were back on serve at 4-3.

Murray stepped up now and on the second point of the game, completely wrong-footed the Serb with a stunning cross-court forehand at the outer reaches of his extremities. Djokovic was on the floor, literally and metaphorically. A service winner made it 30-15 but a Murray forehand floated wide for 30-30. Djokovic then put too much juice on a forehand and it was 40-30 before more Murray brilliance, tracking down a drop shot and sending an on-the-run top-spin forehand over the net to level the set at 4-4. A bewildered Djokovic was shaking his head in a disbelief that was beginning to border on despair.

There was little margin for error now for the Serb as he served again. At 15-15, Murray hared after another drop shot and when Djokovic sent his reply back over the Brit's head, Murray ran backwards, swivelled and blasted a forehand that the Serb could only net. The next point was better still, running from side to side to chase after Djokovic's shots, and then sprinting after a backhand volley, which he again sent down the line with a fabulous forehand pass. Two break points and an off-balance Djokovic netted Murray's return on the first. Utter delirium ensued, Murray clenched his fist and he was on the brink, about to serve for the Wimbledon championship.

THIRD SET STATS:

Aces: Murray 0, Djokovic 2
Double faults: Murray 0, Djokovic 1
1st serves in: Murray 54%, Djokovic 75%
1st serve points won: Murray 58%, Djokovic 52%
Break points won: Murray 3/4, Djokovic 2/5
Winners: Murray 8, Djokovic 14
Unforced errors: Murray 10, Djokovic 11

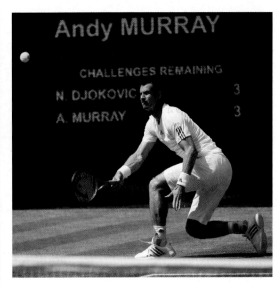

Both men were stretched to their physical limits in a punishing final

THE FINAL GAME, POINT BY POINT

Djokovic long with a backhand after a short exchange, 15-0.

Another punishing baseline rally is punctuated by a backhand drop shot from Djokovic. Yet again, Murray runs after it and flicks a forehand winner down the line. 30-0 and two points away.

A powerful first serve that Djokovic can only send long, 40-0 and three championship points. This is it. This is the moment. Isn't it?

Another fierce first serve, which Djokovic does brilliantly to get back in play as he stretches on the backhand side. The Serb takes the initiative, coming to the net and remaining secure with three successive volleys to stay in the match. 40-15.

With girlfriend Kim Sears visibly shaking as she clasps her hands together in prayer, a Murray second serve sits up and is blasted away by the Djokovic backhand, 40-30.

Murray sends a backhand long and we are back to deuce. The anxiety is tangible.

A tense baseline exchange ends with a Murray forehand into the net. Break point Djokovic.

First serve from Murray which Djokovic sends long. Deuce again.

Djokovic on the offensive again in another long rally but Murray's cross-court backhand from out wide looks like it might be enough. However, Djokovic's low, flicked volley clips the top of the net and drops agonisingly on the Murray side of the net, to gasps of horror from the Centre Court crowd. Break point number two for the Serb.

Murray's nerve will not be broken. Rat-a-tat from the back of the court before the Briton sends a backhand onto the baseline. Djokovic's reply sits up in mid-court and Murray

steps up to flick it away with the forehand. Deuce for the third time. The tension and heat are clearly affecting both players and they are struggling to catch their breath between points.

Murray tries a drop shot of his own but Djokovic gets to it in time and flicks the ball cross-court with a super-cute forehand. The Briton's hands are on his knees and it is break point for a third time.

A big first serve allows Murray to send a flat forehand into the corner. He follows it into the net and, as Djokovic just about keeps the ball in play, Murray puts away an easy volley and clenches his fists at his support team. Deuce for the fourth occasion as chants of "Andy, Andy" ring out.

Yet another breathtaking point. Djokovic sends his man from corner to corner but Murray scurries after the ball to somehow stay in the rally. He sends it up high but Djokovic

looked poised for the kill with an overhead. The Serb's smash is returned with interest by Murray's backhand, Djokovic volleys and the Brit sprints after it again, his forehand down the line having too much heat for his opponent. Absolutely magnificent from Murray, who now has a fourth championship point.

Breathing hard, Murray composes himself amid the bedlam. His first serve finds the target and there are premature cheers from the crowd but Djokovic gets a racquet on it and his reply lands in. Murray sets himself and hits a flat forehand to the backhand corner, and when Djokovic's reply smacks the net, the unbearable tension is released and 77 years of waiting comes to a delirious end. Murray screams with delight as he pumps his fists in triumph. Centre Court and the whole country join him as we enjoyed one of British sport's greatest days.

"I CAN'T EVEN REALLY REMEMBER WHAT HAPPENED, MY MIND WAS EVERYWHERE. AT THE END, I DIDN'T REALLY KNOW WHAT WAS GOING ON"

THE PATH TO
FINAL GLORY

Andy Murray went into Wimbledon 2013 full of confidence following his victory at Queen's in the Aegon Championships. He had missed the French Open due to a back problem but he showed no signs of that at Queen's, and the ease with which he moved over the grass was an indicator that the Wimbledon fortnight would be very special indeed.

This is how he got to the final . . .

FIRST ROUND:

A Murray (GB) 6 6 6
B Becker (GER) 4 3 2

Benjamin Becker briefly troubled Murray early on, but the Scot proved too strong in the end. The pair exchanged many forehand battles from the back of the court, but Murray's superior fitness and experience proved to be too much in the end. A straight sets victory. Murray was up and running.

SECOND ROUND:

A Murray (GB) 6 6 7
Y-H Lu (TPE) 3 3 5

As big guns Rafa Nadal and Roger Federer packed their bags for home, Murray's tilt at the title continued with a victory over Yen-Hsun Lu. Murray lost to Lu at the 2008 Beijing Olympics, but there would be no repeat of that this time. Murray won his second consecutive match without dropping a set.

THIRD ROUND:

A Murray (GB)   6 6 7
T Robredo (SPA) 2 4 5

Once again, Murray underlined his grasscourt skills – and justified his No.2 seeding – with another straight sets win. Tommy Robredo was making his first appearance on Centre Court but he failed to be inspired by his surroundings. Murray cruised into a two-set lead before Robredo finally pushed him harder in the third. Ultimately though it wasn't enough as Murray booked his place in the fourth round.

FOURTH ROUND:

A Murray (GB)   6 7 6
M Youzhny (RUS) 4 6 1

Another match, another straight sets win. This time, though, Murray did face a scare. After winning the first set, Murray then had to dig deep to win the second via a tie-break. His Russian opponent had actually been serving for the second set but Murray broke him. The last set was a formality as Youzhny's spirit was broken and Murray cruised to a 6-1 win.

QUARTER-FINAL:

A Murray (GB)   4 3 6 6 7
F Verdasco (SPA) 6 6 1 4 5

Finally, Murray got the workout he needed. In fact, it was much more than just a workout. Fernando Verdasco pushed Murray to the very limits and took a two-set lead. Murray looked in serious trouble but, inspired by the crowd, he stormed back to take the third set 6-1. He continued to battle in the fourth set and levelled the match before his momentum swept him to victory in three hours and 27 minutes. Murray was back in the Wimbledon semi-finals for the fifth consecutive year.

SEMI-FINAL:

A Murray (GB) **6 6 6 6**
J Janowicz (POL) **7 4 4 3**

So here was the chance, once again, to seal a place in the Wimbledon final. Murray's big-serving opponent, Jerzy Janowicz, had surprised everybody by reaching the last four and he continued to shock by taking the first set via a tie-break. However, Murray remained calm – again buoyed by a wildly supportive audience – and soon hit back. He complained late on in the match when it was decided to close the Centre Court roof, but that did not faze him enough to stop him from securing his place in the final.

THE
MAKING
OF MURRAY

by **Alan Jewell**

Andy Murray's competitive nature was evident from an early age and it was given free expression in a family that was steeped in sport.

Grandfather Roy Erskine was a footballer who played for Stirling Albion and Cowdenbeath and mother Judy was a talented tennis player herself, going on to become a full-time coach.

Her first child, Jamie, was born 15 months before Andy and it's said that the little brother was always striving to keep up with the elder. Within this boisterous environment, the Murray boys spent hours taking part in a series of games that required them to throw, catch, run or balance, developing the skills that would allow both to forge careers in professional tennis.

In 2012, grandmother Shirley Erskine recalled how, as a boy, Andy hated to lose in anything that had a competitive element.

She said: "Andy was a handful as a child. Jamie was much more laid back and when they played board games, the board games would go on the floor if Andy wasn't winning.

"It was a problem at the time but now you look back and recognise the temperament and the desire you need to always win.

"He had a temper on him and would always stamp his foot and say 'I've got to do better, I've got to get better', but he focused that eventually and used his energy to play tennis."

Murray came through a great deal on his journey to Wimbledon and Grand Slam glory, starting during his childhood in the Stirlingshire town of Dunblane.

It's a place that will forever be associated with the horrific murder of 16 schoolchildren and a teacher at Dunblane Primary School in March 1996.

Murray was an eight-year-old pupil of the school at the time and his class were the next due to use the gymnasium where gunman Thomas Hamilton opened fire on helpless five and six year olds. He hid under a desk in the headmaster's office as the shots rang out.

Mum Judy rushed down to the school when she heard about the shootings and had an anxious wait before hearing that her sons were safe. Some of her friends weren't so lucky.

Andy has admitted he struggled to deal with the aftermath of the tragedy. He had attended Hamilton's boys' club and Judy had given him lifts in her car.

Asked about the massacre by Sue Barker in a BBC documentary broadcast on the eve of Wimbledon 2013, a visibly upset Murray struggled to retain his composure before saying: "You have no idea how tough something like that is." Judy revealed that, as he grew older, Andy would ask questions about what happened but Jamie would not.

Although he was a talented footballer, tennis became Andy's priority as the years passed. At the age of 15 he demanded that Judy and father Will allow him to move to Barcelona to train on the clay courts of the Sanchez-Casal Academy, run by former Spanish Davis Cup players Emilio Sanchez and Sergio Casal. Murray had seen another promising teenager, Rafael Nadal, hitting with a Grand Slam winner, Carlos Moya, and felt he needed a greater competitive environment than Britain and the Lawn Tennis Association could offer. Leaving his friends and family behind was a wrench, but Murray's determination to make the best of his talent was fierce.

It was a decision that has paid handsome dividends and he first came to the attention of the sporting public when winning the boys' title at the 2004 US Open. Later that year he was named BBC Young Sports Personality of the Year. Soon after the boy became a man and a magnificent professional career began.

Andy Murray competing in the Wimbledon boys' competition in 2004 and celebrating his US Open junior win later that year (below). On the bottom right, he is pictured, aged 17, with his mum and dad at his side at Wimbledon

Second best: In the background as Roger Federer celebrates winning the Australian Open in 2010

MAKING HEADLINES ALL OVER THE WORLD

Murray's first four Grand Slam finals didn't go according to plan – then came the fairytale of New York . . .

by **Chris McLoughlin**

Roger Federer's assessment of Andy Murray before their US Open final clash at Flushing Meadows in 2008 makes for interesting reading, five years on.

Murray was 21 at the time. He was about to play in his first Grand Slam final. The first Brit to reach such a match since Greg Rusedski in 1997. The opportunity to be Great Britain's first Grand Slam winner since Fred Perry in 1936. History hung heavily on his shoulders, as it has done on every Brit since Perry last triumphed in one of the majors.

Beating world number one Rafa Nadal in a thrilling semi-final had given everyone hope. Federer, unbeaten at Flushing Meadows since 2003, was a different proposition, but the feeling was that he might just be vulnerable. Not as great as he once was. Beatable.

Federer won in straight sets. In less than two hours. 6-2, 7-5, 6-2 – taking his Grand Slam total to 13. But the Swiss star was sporting enough to pay tribute to his disappointed opponent.

"I congratulate Andy," he said. "He's done great these last two weeks. I'm sure we're going to see a lot more of him in the future."

He got that right. Perhaps Murray hadn't played as well on his first truly big occasion as he would've liked, but the young Scot learned a lot from that defeat. "I've got a lot of improving to do if I want to win one of these tournaments," he admitted.

Five years on and Murray holds two of the four Grand Slam titles having played in a further six major finals.

He did it the hard way, though, suffering another three final defeats before breaking his duck.

Federer again stood in his way in Melbourne, 2010. Murray said beforehand that he would have to "play the tennis of my life," to overcome Federer on the hard court, but he didn't. Federer triumphed in straight sets, 6-3, 6-4, 7-6, to win a 16th Grand Slam.

"Congratulations to Roger," said Murray afterwards. "He

was a lot better than me tonight," before adding, as his eyes welled up with tears, "Got great support back home the past two weeks. Sorry I couldn't do it for you tonight."

Federer quickly cut in. "You're too good not to win a Grand Slam, so don't worry about it."

Further disappointment was to follow Down Under 12 months later. This time it wasn't Federer, but Novak Djokovic, on the other side of the net.

The Serb played some scintillating tennis to win 6-4, 6-2, 6-3, but Murray's critics began to circle.

Three Grand Slam finals. Three straight sets defeats.

He was accused of not being aggressive enough. Of being tactically naïve. Of losing his cool too often. Of lacking a top-class coach. Of not turning up.

The criticism stung, but not as much as losing his first Wimbledon final in 2012 did.

To be the first Brit in the All England Club's showpiece occasion since Bunny Austin in 1938 was an achievement in itself, but the pressure on him to end 76 years of hurt was immense, especially as that man Federer was again his opponent, but had slipped down the world rankings – lifting expectation levels higher again.

Now coached by Ivan Lendl, Murray began well. He finally won a set in a Grand Slam final, delighting the crowd by opening with a 6-4 success, but his joy was short-lived. Federer responded by taking the next three sets 7-5, 6-3, 6-4 and the wait for a British Wimbledon champion went on.

"Was it my best chance? I don't know," said Murray. "I lost to a guy that's now won this tournament seven times. It's hard, it's tough to take, but you need to show strength of character to come back from it."

Character is precisely what he showed two months later at Flushing Meadows.

The British number one powered through to his fifth Grand Slam final and, just like in Australia 2011, Djokovic was on court with him.

Having won the boys' singles title there in 2004, with hard courts being his favourite surface and having praised the New York atmosphere in the past, everything was set for Murray to make history.

He flew into a two-set lead, winning the first set 7-6 (12-10) and the second 7-5. Not since Pancho Gonzales in 1949 had anyone rallied from two sets down to win the US Open, but there have been few better battlers on a tennis court than Djokovic. There is no such thing as a lost cause to him.

The man from Belgrade hit back. He won the third set 6-2 then the fourth set 6-3. Suddenly, all the doubts resurfaced. Had Murray blown it? Had he cracked under pressure? What could he do to shift the momentum away from Djokovic?

That's when he showed his true character. A newfound resilience and mental strength. The belief, energy, grit and ability to come back from the baseline brink and play on the front-foot.

Murray broke Djokovic in game one of the final set. He held his serve and broke him again in the third.

The nerves kicked in a little. Djokovic broke back and won his own serve, taking it to 3-2, but after holding his serve to make it 4-2 and winning the seventh game, Murray found himself serving for a first Grand Slam title.

At 40-15 up, Murray launched one final serve. Djokovic's return was long and the Scot sank to his haunches in disbelief. He'd done it. Won a Grand Slam. Ended the 76-year wait. Banished the memories of his previous four final defeats in his 28th Grand Slam tournament.

Andy Murray was the US Open champion. A fairytale of New York had been achieved.

"It's been a long, long journey," he said afterwards. "I don't know if it's disbelief or whatever. I'm very, very happy on the inside; I'm sorry if I'm not showing it as you would like.

"When I was serving for the match, there was a sense of how big a moment that is in British tennis history. More than most British players, I have been asked about it many times when I got close to winning Grand Slams before.

"It's great to have finally done it. I hope it inspires some kids to play tennis and also that it takes away the notion that British tennis players choke or don't win – or it's not a good sport."

Four months later, in January 2013, Murray and Djokovic met again, this time back in Australia.

Murray took the first set 7-6, but with his right foot blistered he was unable to stop the Serb from becoming the first man to win three successive Australian Opens, Djokovic taking the next three sets 7-6, 6-3, 6-2.

Despite the defeat, the Scot was in an upbeat frame of mind.

"The last few months have been the best tennis of my life," he admitted. "I know no-one's ever won a Slam straight after their first and I got close so I have to look at the positives of the last few months. I'm going in the right direction."

On July 7, 2013 at Wimbledon, in his seventh Grand Slam final, Andy Murray reached his destination. His destiny. The pinnacle of tennis.

"Can't believe what's just happened!" he tweeted, still in disbelief.

Roger Federer could. He saw it coming in 2008.

'IT'S GREAT TO HAVE FINALLY DONE IT. I HOPE IT INSPIRES SOME KIDS TO PLAY TENNIS AND ALSO THAT IT TAKES AWAY THE NOTION THAT BRITISH TENNIS PLAYERS CHOKE OR DON'T WIN – OR IT'S NOT A GOOD SPORT'

Home is the hero: In Dunblane after winning the US Open and (top) the press pounce at Heathrow after the New York triumph

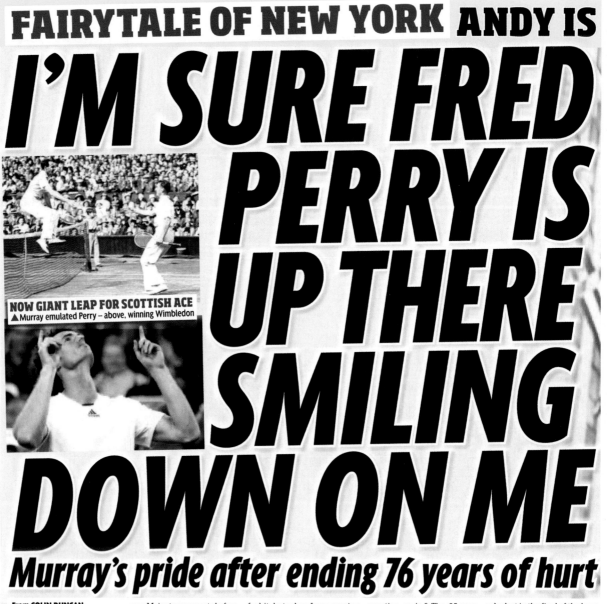

FAIRYTALE OF NEW YORK ANDY IS

I'M SURE FRED PERRY IS UP THERE SMILING DOWN ON ME

NOW GIANT LEAP FOR SCOTTISH ACE
▲ Murray emulated Perry – above, winning Wimbledon

Murray's pride after ending 76 years of hurt

From COLIN DUNCAN
in New York

ANDY MURRAY believes Fred Perry was looking down on him when he finally claimed his place alongside him in the history books.

At the fifth time of asking, the Scotsman exorcised the ghost of past British failures and finally allowed a tennis legend to rest in peace.

Following his epic five-set triumph over Novak Djokovic, the man from Dunblane will no longer live in the shadow of the last British man to win a Grand Slam.

There was a perfect symmetry to their triumphs as it was exactly 76 years to the day that Perry beat Don Budge in the final of the 1936 US Open, two months after he also claimed the last of his Wimbledon victories.

As Murray looked to the New York sky and tried to take in the enormity of his achievement, he was sure Perry would have had a wry smile.

He said: "I never got the chance to meet him. But it would have been nice to have spoken to someone from Britain who had

won Major tournaments before. That definitely would have helped me if I had had the chance.

"I used to wear his clothing line when I was growing up. I'm sure he's smiling up there that someone has finally managed to do it from Britain.

"I'm delighted and I just hope I can see another British player win a Slam in my lifetime."

Perry's name has followed Murray from the moment he won the junior boys title at Flushing Meadows in 2004.

It was a millstone around the Scot's neck but it is one he no longer has to shoulder now he has earned his place among the game's elite.

Yet, while Murray has always played down the burden, he revealed how he felt the weight of history on the fateful final point. He said: "When you're on the court, you don't necessarily

feel it, but when I was serving for the match there was a sense of how big a moment this is in British tennis history.

"So that obviously adds to it. I know more than most what it means. I have been asked about it many times when I got close to winning Grand Slams before.

"Even after I won the Olympics, I still got asked, 'When are you going to win a Grand Slam?'

"It does build pressure. You try not to think about it but when I was serving for the match I realised how important that moment was.

"It's something that hasn't happened for a long time in our country. And I'm proud I managed to achieve it and now I won't get asked that stupid

question again." The 25-year-old laid a number of ghosts to rest as he capped what has been a magnificent summer for British tennis.

A gut-wrenching Wimbledon final defeat by Roger Federer raised the question of whether Murray had the mental strength and self-belief to succeed at the highest level.

Well, his subsequent Olympic triumph when he gained revenge on the Swiss master and his long-awaited moment of glory against Djokovic (left) answered them in the most emphatic fashion.

Throw in the amazing performances of Laura Robson, who beat two Grand Slam champions en-route to the fourth round, and Liam Broady,

who lost in the final of the boys singles, and there are genuine grounds for optimism.

Murray said: "It's great to have finally done it and I hope it inspires some kids to play tennis and also takes away the notion that British tennis players choke or don't win.

"The sport is in a very good place in the UK right now. Laura Robson has done very well, as has Liam Broady."

While Murray was overjoyed to fulfil his lifetime ambition, he was disappointed not to have agreed any forfeits with his training team.

He added: "In the past before some of the Grand Slams I spoke to the guys I work with and said if I win we will do this or we will do that.

"One of them was jumping out of a plane and another was that everyone had to shave their heads. But, unfortunately for this one, we had none.

"It's great to share the win with them because they've been with me from the start.

"Afterwards I saw my girlfriend and my mum and everyone was just in a shock.

"We are so happy but also relieved. It's been a tough journey but we got there in the end."

CAN SERVE WILL SERVE

ANDY MURRAY INSPIRES KIDS EVERYWHERE...

MUM, DAD, I WANT To Be MISERABLE AND HAVE MESSY HAIR!

BY NEIL KERBER AND DAVID BLACK

MURRAY	7-6 7-5 2-6 3-6 6-2	DJOKOVIC
5	Aces	7
4	Double faults	5
65 %	1st serves in	62 %
62 %	1st serve points won	63 %
48 %	2nd serve points won	42 %
132 MPH	Fastest serve	128 MPH
111 MPH	Average 1st serve speed	116 MPH
83 MPH	Average 2nd serve speed	91 MPH
47 %	Break points won	50 %
31	Winners	40
56	Unforced errors	65
160	Total points won	155

US OPEN FINAL STATS

MAJOR STAR AT THE 5TH ATTEMPT

SILVER LINING
Murray with his trophy the day after his triumph in New York

▲ **HANDY SUPPORT** Ferguson

FAN FERGIE IN SALUTE TO CHAMP

From COLIN DUNCAN

ANDY MURRAY knew he could not fail to win the US Open with Sir Alex Ferguson in his corner.

The Manchester United manager is famous for his 'hairdryer' rollickings for his superstar players.

But he was with Team Murray on Monday night, signalling to his fellow Scot to keep calm.

Murray said: "I was looking at the guys in the box because I needed to get myself pumped up in the fifth set and that helped me.

"It was great to have someone like Sir Alex around and get to chat to him. It was pretty cool. That is always going to inspire you.

"All of the other guys spoke to him and said he was really good fun and was very happy for me."

Fergie said: "I'm really proud for the boy. That was a real test of a champion for me.

"I love watching tennis and it was more nerve-wracking than a Premier League match. I'm usually in control of my own situation but I wasn't in control here."

▲ **TOPS** Federer is current No.1

READY TO BE RULER

FROM BACK PAGE

world No.1. I can't say this year it's necessarily possible for me to do it because I didn't have a particularly good clay court season and had too many losses in the other tournaments.

"But becoming No.1 and winning more Majors is the next step.

"To do that, you need to be consistent through the whole year.

"That's something that Novak, Roger Federer and Rafa Nadal have done incredibly well in the last few years.

"It is difficult for guys to get up there but I'm definitely going to try."

SEAN WINNER ▲ Connery cheered on Murray, who was with actor Matthew Perry the next day before showing off cup

GOLDEN BOY

by **Chris Brereton**

As a packed Centre Court hushed itself to silence, Andy Murray – covered in sweat and with the toil written across his face – served for the match.

The sun was shining, a tennis superstar at the other end of the court was ready to face Murray's huge serve, the tension and excitement was palpable, both in the stands and on the streets of Great Britain.

A nation expected.

And then, finally, Murray had done it.

He had won an Olympic gold medal.

The seeds of Murray's Wimbledon glory in 2013 were sown at Centre Court 11 months earlier during the Olympics.

Just 28 days before his Olympic final against Roger Federer, Murray had been beaten by the Swiss great in the 2012 Wimbledon final.

That match was Murray's fourth Grand Slam final and, just like the other three, it ended in defeat.

The chance for revenge was just what Murray needed. And he took it.

In fact, he did more than take it. He crushed Federer – the best player on planet Earth for the last decade, if not ever.

Murray beat Federer 6-2, 6-1, 6-4 on that bright, perfect August afternoon and the sense of relief, and excitement, that victory brought has made an epic difference to his game.

Since that gold medal-winning performance, Murray has been in three more Grand Slam finals – the 2012 US Open, the 2013 Australian Open and, of course, Wimbledon 2013 – and he has won two of the three.

It is no coincidence.

Beating Federer, on home soil, helped Murray's confidence to sky-rocket.

No longer would he consider himself just a bridesmaid.

It was time to walk up the aisle himself.

Murray has publicly acknowledged how important the Team GB success was at London 2012 and it also helped cement him as a Centre Court favourite.

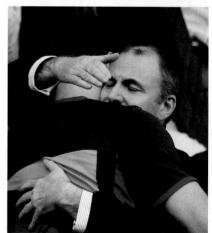

GB hero: Beating Roger Federer and winning an Olympic gold medal helped Andy to really believe he could step up to the next level at Wimbledon

ANDY'S WIMBLEDON JOURNEY

From his first appearance in 2005 to his victory in 2013, Andy Murray's Wimbledon story has had it all – highs, lows, tears and cheers

by **Alan Jewell**

Andy Murray was a callow, gangly 18-year-old with a world ranking of 312 when his Wimbledon story began in June 2005.

Back then, he was not the centre of attention for British tennis fans as Tim Henman and Greg Rusedski, aged 30 and 31 respectively, were still carrying home hopes. It was a sign of things to come that in his debut Grand Slam, Murray went further than both of them.

In his first round match (only his fifth ATP Tour encounter) he dismissed Switzerland's George Bastl in straight sets on Court Two, three years after Bastl had ended Pete Sampras's Wimbledon career on the same court.

In round two he faced 14th seed Radek Stepanek and Murray's pre-match verdict was: "I should lose pretty comfortably". He couldn't have been more wrong, wowing the crowd on Court One with another fabulous display that belied his youth and inexperience. He won again in straight sets, 6-4, 6-4, 6-4. As Henman and Rusedski were beaten at the same stage, a banner in the crowd said it all: "Andrew Murray – A New Hope".

Murray got his first taste of Centre Court in round three, facing 2002 finalist David Nalbandian. Watched by fellow Scot Sir Sean Connery, Murray won the first two sets and served for the match in the fourth but, at that stage, he did not have the stamina to match his skill and suffered an attack of cramp. Nalbandian eventually prevailed in five sets but Murray had served notice of his exciting potential.

Twelve months later his ranking was into the top 50 and he reached the third round again, facing third seed (and finalist for the previous two years) Andy Roddick on Centre Court. Murray was superb and won in straight sets, 7-6, 6-4, 6-4. However, two days later he experienced a letdown in round four and was beaten in three sets by talented Cypriot Marcos Baghdatis.

A wrist injury forced him to miss the 2007 tournament, a huge disappointment for all British fans, but he was able to watch older brother Jamie win the mixed doubles title alongside Jelena Jankovic.

By 2008 Henman and Rusedski had retired so the focus was all on Murray, seeded 12th. He reached the quarter-finals of a Grand Slam for the first time thanks to a thrilling win over Frenchman Richard Gasquet in the fourth round. Gasquet served for the match in the third set but Murray broke back, won the subsequent tiebreak and stormed through the final two sets to win in a fevered atmosphere as the light faded at 9.30pm. However, in the last eight he didn't have the strength to see off Rafael Nadal, losing in straight sets to the Spaniard who went on to take the title that year.

A year later Murray's gradual progression continued as he made the semi-finals for the first time. Seeded third, he was actually the bookies' favourite to beat Roddick in the last four but the American was the better player on the day and won 6-4, 4-6, 7-6, 7-6.

In 2010 and 2011 Murray reached the semi-finals again but on both occasions Nadal had too much for him. In the second of those matches Murray actually began the better

A fresh-faced Murray pictured shortly before his Wimbledon debut in 2005

Right: Murray's first Wimbledon came to an end in the third round after losing to David Nalbandian

Murray may have lost but his will to win caught the attention and imagination of the British sporting public

How the Daily Mirror reported on the
new sensation in British tennis

and led by a set and 2-1, with 15-30 on the Nadal serve. However, a missed mid-court forehand appeared to derail him and the Spaniard won seven games in a row on the way to a four-set victory.

In many ways the 2012 Wimbledon championships was a watershed for Murray (no pun intended). Nadal's shocking loss in the second round opened up the draw for him, and he took full advantage. In the last eight he had to dig deep to overcome another Spaniard, David Ferrer, who served for a two-set lead before Murray raised his game to win in four. In the semi-final Jo-Wilfried Tsonga was also beaten in four sets as Murray became the first British man to reach the Wimbledon final since Bunny Austin in 1938. The emotional scenes afterwards demonstrated that this was an achievement in itself.

In the final he faced the king of Centre Court, Roger Federer, who was seeking his seventh title at SW19. Federer had beaten Murray in two previous Grand Slam finals but Murray actually had a winning record against the Swiss master.

The Briton made a fast start, breaking serve in the first game and although Federer got back on terms, another break in the ninth game allowed Murray to serve out the set.

Murray remained the dominant player as the second set progressed and created four break points, including two at 4-4, but was unable to take them and Federer raised his game from nowhere with Murray serving at 5-6 to break and level at one set all.

Left: Agony for Murray in 2006 as Marcos Baghdatis ended his run in the fourth round. It was a subdued loss which surprised many, especially as Murray had beaten Andy Roddick in the previous round

Murray salutes Baghdatis at the end of their fourth-round tie

➤ Early in the third set the rain began to fall, forcing the closure of the Centre Court roof. The change in conditions suited Federer's attacking style as he could go for the lines without worrying about the wind. An epic 20-minute game with Murray serving at 2-3 in the third proved decisive as Federer eventually broke through on his tenth break point and went on to take the set 6-3.

Murray fought valiantly until the end, but a single break of serve was enough for Federer in the fourth as he won the title again, prevailing 4-6, 7-5, 6-3, 6-4.

Through the years it had often been a slightly awkward relationship between player and crowd as Wimbledon spectators found it difficult to fully embrace the shy, diffident and volatile Murray. But a bond was finally sealed on this day. His touching, emotional speech, delivered through tears and with a quivering voice, captured hearts on court and among the millions of television viewers.

When the dust settled and tears dried, he was able to reflect on a wonderful tournament and a performance in the final in which he could feel proud. Twelve months later, by then a Grand Slam winner, he was, joyously, able to go that one step further.

Murray with his girlfriend, Kim Sears. He had to miss Wimbledon in 2007 due to a wrist injury

After a thrilling come-from-behind victory over Richard Gasquet in the fourth round in 2008, Rafael Nadal ended his run at the quarter-final stage

Murray serving in the fourth set against Andy Roddick

Above: Roddick ended Murray's Wimbledon dream in 2009 as the American won their semi-final clash 6-4, 4-6, 7-6, 7-6. The signs were good though. Murray was clearly getting stronger, fitter and was no longer daunted by the big stage

Right: Murray acknowledges Roddick's efforts at the end of their match

Another semi-final, another loss. Centre Court could not will Murray to victory over Rafael Nadal in 2010

Nadal hits a backhand return in their 2011 semi-final

Left: A downhearted Murray can see the end coming against Nadal

Right: Murray again has to shake an opponent's hand at the end of a losing semi-final

Above and right: The most painful loss of them all. The 2012 final saw Roger Federer beat Murray in four sets

Murray puts on a brave face as he poses for photographs with Swiss great Federer

It was a name we heard
on countless occasions
at every Wimbledon as
a succession of British
players tried and failed to
emulate his achievement.
Fred Perry was a great
champion in his own right

PERRY V

MURRAY

If Fred Perry had still been alive, and if he had been sat in Centre Court at Wimbledon on Sunday, July 7, 2013, the chances are he would have sat there shaking his head in disbelief.

The noise, the cheering, the size and shape of the racquets, the flashbulbs and the cameras; the tennis world, just like the wider world, has moved on since Perry's heyday.

The most daunting statistic in British sport used to be the annual addition of another year onto the "how long is it since a Brit won Wimbledon?" question.

First it was a decade. That that became half a century, then 60 years, then 70, then, finally, 77 years.

In other words, an entire lifetime passed between Perry's victory in 1936 and Murray's win this year.

To put in another way; Perry won his Wimbledon titles while wearing trousers.

That is how long ago it was.

That is how much the world has changed.

In 1936, Britain was gripped by the abdication crisis as Edward VIII stepped down to make way for his brother "Bertie", or King George VI.

World War Two was still three years away, the Spanish Civil War was raging and the Spitfire was given its maiden flight.

At the time, it would have taken hours for the news of Perry's victory to circle the globe.

When Murray won Wimbledon, within minutes his Twitter account was updated.

"Can't believe what's just happened!!!!!!!" Murray wrote.

Perry would practically have needed a quill, some ink and the Royal Mail to convey the same thoughts.

But, finally, the wait is over and the ghost of Perry can be put to rest.

One final way of looking at the dearth of British winners is this: If the nation has to wait as long again for another victory to cheer, we will have to keep our fingers crossed until 2090.

However, with Murray reaching the peak years of his career, the chances of needing to hang on that long seem very slim indeed...

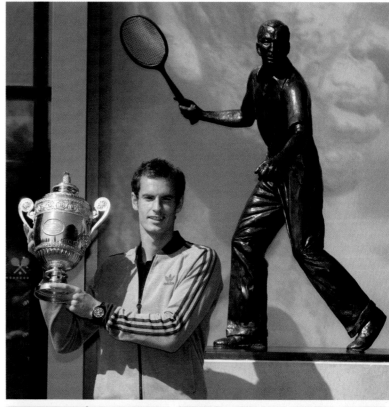

PERRY'S WIMBLEDON WINS

1934
Perry beat Jack Crawford (AUS) 6–3, 6–0, 7–5
The first of Perry's three consecutive Wimbledon titles arrived in 1934.

He faced Jack Crawford, the brilliant Australian player who had won at SW19 the year before.

Crawford was known for taking a shot of whisky during the match if events on court were getting tense. He had little to cheer about in this contest as Perry swept to victory in straight sets.

1935
Perry beat Gottfried von Cramm 6–2, 6–4, 6–4
Perry returned to Wimbledon the following year and successfully defended his title against Gottfried von Cramm, a German tennis star and twice the winner of the French Open.

Again though, Perry had few problems as he saw off the German in straight sets.

1936
Perry beat Gottfried von Cramm 6–1, 6–1, 6–0
Perry's hat-trick opportunity came up against von Cramm again and Perry made sure he did not miss out, losing just two games across the entire match as von Cramm was routed.

By 1936, von Cramm had become a very reluctant poster boy for the Nazi party but he wanted nothing to do with Adolf Hitler and ended up fighting on the Eastern front during World War Two as a punishment for refusing to endorse the Nazi regime.

ANDY MURRAY'S
SEVENTH HEAVEN

The number seven is clearly Murray's
lucky number. *Here's why...*

The last British winner of a
Wimbledon singles title was
Virginia Wade in 1977

Andy broke Novak
Djokovic's serve in
the 7th game of all
three sets and 7
times in total

The last Scot of
either sex to win
a Wimbledon
singles title was
Harold Mahoney,
117 years ago

77

...years since Fred Perry
became the last Brit to win the
Wimbledon men's singles title

7TH

Wimbledon 2013 was
Andy Murray's 7th
Grand Slam final

7 Days

Murray was born
exactly 7 days before
Djokovic in 1987

07.07

His victory came on 7/7, the
7th day of the 7th month

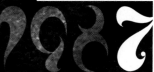

THE BRITS WHO MISSED OUT

When Scotland's Andy Murray beat Novak Djokovic in the men's singles final at Wimbledon, it ended a 77-year wait for a British winner. During that time, a number of other Brits carried the hopes of a nation in their racquet bags. Some, such as John Lloyd, Buster Mottram, Andrew Castle, Jeremy Bates, Mark Petchey and Chris Bailey never troubled the engraver, but eight others came closer to netting the greatest prize in tennis . . .

Bunny Austin
Finalist: 1932, 1938 Semi-finalist: 1937
Quarter-finalist: 1939

Beaten in the 1932 final by America's Ellsworth Vines, Henry Wilifred 'Bunny' Austin famously became the first tennis player to wear shorts in 1933 when he asked his tailor to find an alternative to the sweat-sodden cricket flannels that were weighing him down on court. Although he was part of Great Britain's quadruple Davis Cup winning side of 1933-1936, he lived in three-times winner Fred Perry's shadow between 1934 and 1936 as far as Wimbledon was concerned. Austin followed defeat at the 1937 semi-final stage by reaching his second final in 1938 only to be beaten by another American, Don Budge, 6-1, 6-0, 6-3. He only made it to the quarter-finals when number one seed in 1939 – his 10th appearance in the last eight at the age of 33 – but that was to be his last championship at SW19 before his retirement. Austin died in 2000 on his 94th birthday and, until Andy Murray in 2012, was the last Brit to reach a Wimbledon final for 74 years.

Bunny Austin

Donald MacPhail
Quarter-finalist: 1938

Born on Christmas Day, 1911, the Glaswegian made his Wimbledon debut in 1933, but only once did he enjoy a prolonged run in the tournament, reaching the last eight in 1938. The Scot was beaten that year by Yugoslav Franjo Punec, denying him a crack at eventual winner Don Budge in the semi-final and then Bunny Austin in the final.

Tony Mottram
Quarter-finalist: 1948

Having made his Wimbledon debut in 1939, Coventry-born Mottram had to wait another seven years to participate in the tournament again due to World War Two and in 1948 he became Britain's first post-war quarter-finalist. A year earlier, he'd reached the men's doubles final, partnered by Australian Bill Sidwell, only to lose in straight sets to American pair Bob Falkenburg and Jack Kramer. Mottram was on course to meet Falkenburg in the 1948 singles final but ran into number three seed Gardnar Mulloy in the last eight, who beat him 6-2, 1-6, 7-5, 6-1. That was as close as he got to winning Wimbledon although he fared better than his son, Christopher 'Buster' Mottram, whose best run took him to the fourth round in 1982.

Bobby Wilson
Quarter-finalist: 1958, 1959, 1961, 1963

A British junior champion at the age of 15, Wilson caused quite a stir in 1958 when he reached the Wimbledon quarter-finals unseeded – without dropping a set – and gave number one ranked Aussie Ashley Cooper the fright of his life, coming back from two sets down to level matters at 2-2 before only losing the decider 7-5. By the time he returned 12 months later he was seeded four and qualified for the last eight again only to lose in straight sets to another Australian, Roy Emerson. In 1961 he knocked out number one seed Neale Fraser, but was defeated in the quarters by eventual runner-up Chuck McKinley and his last-eight jinx continued in 1963 when McKinley, who went on to win the title, was again his opponent. Hendon-born Bobby was 27 by then and although he continued to play in the singles at Wimbledon until 1970, his best years were behind him.

Mike Sangster
Semi-finalist: 1961

Hailing from Devon, right-handed Sangster played football for Torquay United as a youngster but turned to tennis and made his Wimbledon debut aged just 17 in 1958. Noted for a big serve that was recorded as reaching 154mph, he caught the imagination of the public in 1961 when he became the first Brit to reach the semi-finals at Wimbledon since Bunny Austin in 1938. Chuck McKinley, who had beaten fellow Brit Bobby Wilson in the quarter-final, was Sangster's opponent and although it was a hard-fought contest, the American prevailed 6-4, 6-4, 8-6. Sangster also reached the semi-final of the US Open in 1961 and the last four of the French Open in 1963, making him, at the time, only the second Brit to have reached the semi-final of all three tournaments alongside Fred Perry. A British record holder for the most Davis Cup appearances, Sangster's last Wimbledon was in 1969 and he died of a heart-attack at the age of 44 in 1985.

Roger Taylor

Roger Taylor
Semi-finalist: 1967, 1970, 1973

A winner of six singles and 10 doubles titles during his career, Sheffield-born Taylor was Great Britain's best hope of ending the Wimbledon drought in the 1970s but was never able to progress beyond the semi-final. The left-hander first made it to the last four in 1967, but was beaten by Germany's Wilhelm Bungert in a thrilling five-setter, 6-4, 6-8, 2-6, 6-4, 6-4. Despite a shock win over defending champion Rod Laver in 1970, another semi-final defeat followed, this time to Aussie Ken Rosewall. In 1973, when seeded three, he famously beat 17-year-old sensation Bjorn Borg in the quarter-final after volunteering to replay a point that the Swede had disputed with the umpire. That set Taylor up with a semi-final against Czech Jan Kodes, but he lost an epic match 8-9, 9-7, 5-7, 6-4, 7-5 and never came close to reaching the final again before his retirement in 1980.

Greg Rusedski
Quarter-finalist: 1997

Although he was born in Montreal and represented Canada until he was 22, Rusedski gained British citizenship in 1995 and two years later became the first Brit to reach a Grand Slam final since Bunny Austin when he was beaten in the US Open final by Pat Rafter. Earlier that year, Rusedski had turned in his best display at Wimbledon, progressing to the quarter-finals unseeded after a notable first round victory against Mark Philippoussis. Despite a disappointing defeat to Cedric Pioline in the last eight, Rusedski was named as BBC Sports Personality for 1997 but never performed to the same level at Wimbledon again.

Tim Henman
Semi-finalist: 1998, 1999, 2001, 2002
Quarter-finalist: 1996, 1997, 2003, 2004

For almost a decade, Henman epitomised British sport's 'so near, yet so far' era, looking like he could finally end the wait for success at SW19 only for his challenges to end in glorious failure. After quarter-final defeats in 1996 (to Todd Martin) and 1997 (to Michael Stich), he reached consecutive semi-finals only to be beaten twice by Pete Sampras. After overcoming Roger Federer in the 2001 quarter-final he was just two points away from reaching the final, but eventually succumbed to wildcard winner Goran Ivanisevic in a rain-affected semi-final. Henman made the semis again in 2002, this time going down to Lleyton Hewitt in straight sets, and by the time he suffered quarter-final defeats to Sebastien Grosjean (2003) and Mario Ancic (2004) it was apparent that it was never going to be the Oxford-born right-hander's year. Hugely popular with the Wimbledon crowds who'd get caught up in Henmania and yell "C'mon Tim" between points, the Aorangi Terrace outside the newly rebuilt Court One was dubbed 'Henman Hill' in the late '90s due to the large swathes of fans who would watch his matches on the big screen there. These days it is known as Murray Mound.

Tim Henman

A FAMILY AFFAIR

When Andy Murray followed in the famous footsteps of Pat Cash and clambered his way up to thank his friends and family after his epic Wimbledon win, his smile was as big as SW19 itself. And for a good reason. Murray's box was crammed with those who helped get him into the final, get him into his astonishing physical condition and get him into the history books.

by **Chris Brereton**

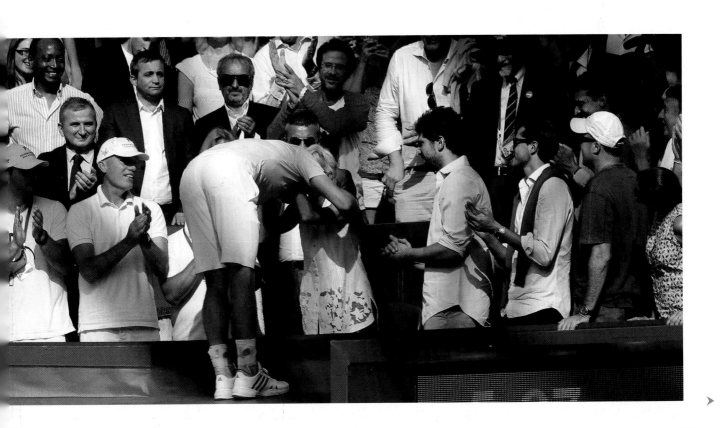

When Novak Djokovic sent the ball crashing into the Wimbledon net, handing the 2013 title to Andy Murray, the Scot's mum, Judy, burst into floods of tears.

The very public display of emotion was a rarity from a woman who has been the leading light and guiding influence behind Murray's ascendancy to the top table of tennis.

Murray is never more than a point or two away from looking up at the box during a match, searching for and receiving the reassurance from his mum that he is happy enough to admit he needs.

His mum "is the one person who gets me, who understands me really well," according to Murray and his Wimbledon victory – just like his US Open win before it – was as much Judy's as his.

Judy clearly plays every point along with her son and he often looks up to her if his self-belief is waning and his confidence dented.

"I know that when Andy looks up, he wants to see some kind of positive reaction," Judy said.

"You will never find me doing anything negative like shaking my head. Never, ever."

Her tearful reaction, as understandable as it was, came as a surprise because Judy does not, generally, do emotion.

She sits courtside for every match her youngest son plays and is usually a combination of poker-faced resilience and super positivity.

She has been the rock behind Andy, and his brother Jamie, since they first picked up tennis racquets as toddlers, pouring her time and effort into helping them thrive and get on.

Judy, and Andy's father Willie, found the money to send Murray to the Sanchez-Casal Academy in Barcelona as a youngster in a bid to help him squeeze every ounce out of his talent.

Allowing Murray to move to Spain to fulfil his potential must have been heart-breaking for a mother who was so close to her son.

However, the gamble has paid off.

And paid off spectacularly.

Amid the maelstrom following his epic Wimbledon win, Murray almost forgot to give his mum a hug when he climbed up to thank his support team.

But, finally, he found her among the cheering masses, leant down and wrapped his mum up in a sweaty, teary embrace.

The hug told its own story as Murray paid the best possible tribute to the woman who has been there from the start.

Mum Judy gets a tearful hug and kiss from her victorious son

Andy with his older brother Jamie at the opening ceremony of the Beijing Olympics in 2008

A hug for dad, Willie, after Andy had won the gold medal at the Olympic Games in London in 2012

HIS TENNIS FAMILY...

IVAN LENDL

The Czech-born tennis great – himself the winner of eight Grand Slam titles – became Murray's full-time coach in 2012. Lendl has worked hard at toughening Murray's mental approach and although the pair are both known for being stubborn, their partnership has blossomed from the very start.

Murray has often paid tribute to the way Lendl has strengthened every aspect of his game and did so again after beating Djokovic. "He believed in me when a lot of people didn't and stuck by me through some tough losses. He has been very patient and I'm just happy I've managed to do it for him," Murray said.

Head coach: Ivan Lendl

JEZ GREEN

In the past five years, Murray has gone from pale looking weakling to arguably the strongest man in world tennis. The change in his body has been phenemonal and his fitness coach Green can take a lot of credit for the transformation.

Green pushes Murray to his physical limit with endless hours of fitness training and also makes him eat huge quantities of food – especially protein – in order to make his body grow.

Fitness coach: Jez Green

Kim Sears screams and jumps for joy as Andy wins the Wimbledon title

➤ **Nobody screamed louder than Kim Sears, Murray's girlfriend, when he overcame Novak Djokovic to win the 2013 Wimbledon title.**

Murray and Kim first met in 2005 at the French Open and, apart from a brief break in 2009, they have been a long-term item.

And there is no doubt that Kim brings calm – and a hint of glamour – into Murray's life.

Kim's father, Nigel, is a renowned tennis coach and has been the head of the women's section of the Lawn Tennis Association so she understands the rigours of the game better than most partners.

Murray's mother, Judy, has called her "the best thing to have happened to Andy" and that is as good an endorsement as any.

Although Sears is a permanent fixture at Murray's big matches – she never misses a second of any Grand Slam occasion – she has no desire to be a tennis "WAG", preferring instead to concentrate on building up her business as an artist who paints portraits of pets.

Her and Murray live together in a Surrey mansion they share with their dogs, Maggie May and Rusty.

Murray has been repeatedly asked about when he is going to pop the question and although he insists there is no rush for the couple to get married, the bookies have slashed the odds on the duo marrying following his sensational Wimbledon win.

Andy's mum Judy (left) has described Kim (right) as the best thing to happen to the tennis star

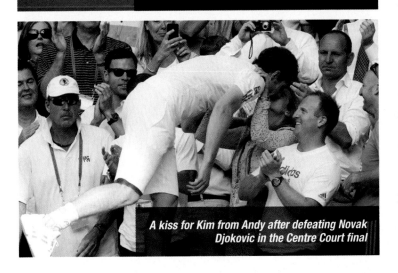

A kiss for Kim from Andy after defeating Novak Djokovic in the Centre Court final

DANNY VALLVERDU

The Venezuelan was once a singles player himself – although he never set the world alight – but he has become an indispensable ally to Murray. The pair met as youngsters at the Sanchez-Casal academy in Spain and are firm friends. He helps coach Murray alongside Lendl and is also one of Murray's hitting partners.

Coach/ Hitting partner: Danny Valverdu

MATT GENTRY

Gentry is Murray's agent, alongside Louise Irving.

Agent: Matt Gentry

MATT LITTLE

As well as Jez Green, Little is also responsible for Murray's strength and conditioning.

The early part of Murray's career was overshadowed by injury but Little's expertise – and the stretching programme he has devised for Murray – has meant injuries have become less of an issue.

Conditioning coach: Matt Little

FACES IN THE CROWD

MUSIC
Ronnie Wood

TV & FILM

Steve Coogan

Bradley Cooper & Gerard Butler

Alex Salmond &
Ed Miliband

David
Cameron

POLITICS

SPORT

Victoria
Beckham

FASHION

Sir
Chris
Hoy

Coleen & Wayne Rooney

HISTORY IN THE MAKING

Murray salutes the fans as the moment is realised

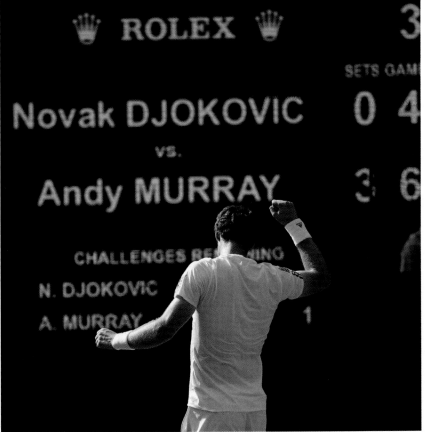

VICTORY IS TWEET

Oh my God. What a match, what a player. Inspiring a Nation. Andy Murray!! Ya Beauty

Ewan McGregor

What a fighter! What a talent. What a man. What a winner! @andy_murray Wimbledon champion! Congratulations!

Gary Lineker

Congratulations @andy--murray! What a match, you've made us all proud! #Wimbledon

Nick Clegg

Congratulations Andy Murray. A historic and amazing moment for him and for the whole country

Ed Miliband

Congratulations to my one time doubles partner

Boris Johnson

Unbelievable. What a fantastic story. Magnificent. What fantastic dignity from the loser. Off to celebrate. Ya beauty

Kenny Dalglish

Get in Andy Murray!! What a champion's performance. And what a gent Novak Djokovic is. Great match. Great winner.

Ant And Dec

This pool of sportsmen that are despised is shrinking with that victory by Murray. I'm starting to get lonely... #comebackandy

Joey Barton

#So buzzing @andy_murray for prime minister!!!

David Haye

Congratulations Andy Murray Awesome!!

Joe Calzaghe

Pretty sure @andy_murray might have to change his twitter name to @sirandymurray Well played

Andy Roddick

Wimbledon Champion!! Well Done @andy_murray! Brilliant!!

Jessica Ennis

That was great to see!! Well done Andy Murray

Danny Cipriani

Slazenger.

*Murray acknowledges his support
as he heads off to collect the trophy*

Supporters show their allegiance during a memorable day for British tennis

Fans in Dunblane cheer on their hometown hero

"SITTING AT HOME YOU'RE NOT THERE, SO YOU CAN CURSE AND SWEAR AND KICK TABLES AND DO ALL THE THINGS YOU CAN'T DO WHEN EVERYONE IS WATCHING YOU ON CENTRE COURT. IT REMINDS ME OF HOW I USED TO PLAY. SOME OF THOSE DINKY THINGS HE DOES ALL THE TIME NOW, HE GOT FROM ME"

ROY ERSKINE, ANDY MURRAY'S GRANDFATHER

MATS WILANDER, WINNER OF SEVEN GRAND SLAM TITLES:

"I think Andy Murray can win six, seven, eight, nine, 10 majors. The only man that can stop him is Novak Djokovic. These two here are going to decide who gets ahead in the history books. I hope they both decide this is a rivalry that's just going to grow and become great on all the different surfaces, in all four majors."

The men's Wimbledon champion safeguards his prize before giving it some close examination

BORIS BECKER, THREE-TIME WIMBLEDON CHAMPION:

"You cannot underestimate the impact of Ivan Lendl. You can't give him enough credit. He never shows any emotion but today he was actually a bit agitated. I haven't seen him like that. He is human after all. I am sure Andy has won it in his mind a thousand times but it's reality now. You can't applaud him loud enough for what he has done. The next goal is to be the world number one and he already holds two Grand Slams. He needs to do everything he can to get that number one spot. There is a serious threat that he can do it."

Murray seals his Wimbledon triumph with a kiss

JOHN MCENROE, THREE-TIME WIMBLEDON CHAMPION:

"He was getting closer and, to me, the Olympics was the big difference. He had to get back off the mat after losing to Federer last year and that forced him to get back on the court quicker. All of a sudden the crowd really got behind him, realised they could make a difference and they did. He won the US Open, so that took a little bit of pressure off coming into this year's Wimbledon. The draw opened up and it was like 'he's got to get at least to the final'. He did that

and then he was able to play up to his ability. It was very hot - a lot of strain and stress on both guys. I'd be surprised if he doesn't win at least six majors. He's come into his own and there's a lot to look forward to. This is a new face who has stepped up in a big way. It's clearly important for all of tennis, but here [in Britain] it's monumental. Every year people ask the same questions - now he never has to hear Fred Perry's name again."

DAVID PERRY,
SON OF FRED PERRY:

"It's been 77 years. The legacy has been there but time goes on and I am thrilled that a British individual has finally won Wimbledon again. It's great for British tennis. Andy has worked his way up there. He deserves it. It's wonderful that he has won it and that he has played the way that he has. He has been playing beautiful tennis. I think my father would have said, 'Do you know what, it's time for somebody else to have the title'. It has been a long time. It had to come, it was just a matter of time. It's great that Andy has done it. You have to give him credit. Andy is a great player. I watched the match. I am sorry it didn't go to four sets or five sets because you want a Wimbledon final to be fantastic. But Andy has finally got himself mentally over the line and now who knows how many he can win."

PENNY PERRY,
DAUGHTER OF FRED PERRY:

"I'm not sure what I was thinking. I was watching in a bit of a daze, expecting the inevitable. I am stunned. Dad would have been stunned. We, as a family and the nation, have spent so long waiting, it is almost wow, now it has happened we are not too sure how to react. Fred was fiercely patriotic and this is fabulous for Britain. It is fantastic for British tennis. He spent 40, 50, 60 years being asked every year 'where is the next Brit coming from?'. He couldn't answer then and today we have found it. I think it is amazing, it is fabulous, congratulations to him."

Murray celebrates on the balcony of Centre Court as he draws applause from an adoring public

Centre Court - South West Hall

VICTORY IS TWEET

Get in @andy_murray played the no 1 off the park. Well done mate #ace
Ricky Hatton

Well done @andy_murray deserved it mate!!
Jack Wilshere

Magnificent Britains @andy_murray going out playing tennis now!!!!
Phil Neville

Congratulations to @andy_murray and his family. Wonderful day at #wimbledon!! So proud to be British!
Victoria Beckham

Andy Murray displayed traits of great fighters and that is intestinal fortitude and that killer instinct! Congrats Andy!
Sugar Ray Leonard

A big congratulations to @andy_murray and Marion on the incredible achievements this weekend
Maria Sharapova

Congratulations to @andy_murray - Dreams do come true; Herculean effort to win under that pressure!!!
Chris Evert

Congratulations @andy_murray. Magnificent achievement and deserved #Wimbledon Champion
Celtic Football Club

The only way Andy Murray can fail to win Sports Personality of the Year is if David Beckham finds a cure for malaria in the next five months
Jeremy Vine

Andy Murray, you champion, well done son
Russell Crowe

Andy Murray winning Wimbledon is my 1966 World Cup moment. What an incredible thing to witness
Jimmy Carr

RT @andy_murray: Can't believe what's just happened!<--Well deserved. Strange that no1 called me 2deliver the trophy 2 u tho
Lennox Lewis

Andy Murray ends Wimbledon curse on Brits with some outstanding tennis. Congratulations--- and also to Ivan Lendl for a job well done
Jimmy Connors

TIM HENMAN,
FORMER BRITISH NUMBER ONE:

"It's a remarkable achievement for him and something we are proud of. Andy had this belief in his heart of hearts that he would win it. He had some huge disappointment with losing 12 months ago but deep down he knew he could do this and this is going to be one of many more grand slams for Andy Murray."

SIR CHRIS HOY,
RETIRED OLYMPIC CHAMPION CYCLIST:

"It has been an absolute privilege to have been in the box with crew and family and friends. It was a special moment to share with them and they must have wondered if it was ever going to happen. It looks like a walkover with a three-set win but it was a real battle. Andy took everything Djokovic threw at him. Now after 77 years, we can celebrate a British winner at Wimbledon. You can see the difference the Olympics win had for him, it gave him the extra confidence. It is an amazing achievement and there is no reason why he can't be a multiple winner of Wimbledon."

Murray shows off the greatest prize in tennis to the world's media

ROGER DRAPER, CHIEF EXECUTIVE OF THE LTA:

"Andy has provided British tennis with its finest moment, on the world's greatest tennis stage. Just as he did last year, at the Olympics and US Open, Andy has proved himself to be an inspirational role model, and he has given British tennis a fantastic opportunity to get more people playing tennis."

Murray with the Wimbledon trophy at the Champion's Ball and with his mother, Judy (left)

DAVID CAMERON, PRIME MINISTER:

"The noise was incredible, it was intense. Every point was exciting, there was so many breaks and break backs. In the Royal Box we were shouting and hugging, it was so emotional because we have waited so long for a champion. It was an amazing day for Brtiish tennis and for Britain. It felt like the Olympics. The whole country was watching. Andy has dedicated his life to this, and he produced a performance that was exquisite. On behalf of everyone in Britain, well done Andy. Congratulations, you have lifted us all. He is an amazing player, he showed today that he has brilliant technique and incredible courage. Djokovic is an artist of comebacks, but Andy was brilliant."

David Cameron and Alex Salmond show their support, and (below) the Prime Minister goes through the emotions

ALEX SALMOND, SCOTTISH FIRST MINISTER:

"Andy's determination to win was visible in every point and he delivered an outstanding result in a real clash of tennis titans. His phenomenal performance against the world number one displayed incredible physical prowess and depths of mental fortitude. The shouts of 'Come on Andy' were ringing all the way from Dunblane to SW19. Last year Andy Murray won the hearts of Wimbledon, this year he has won the championship and on today's form there will be many more victories to come. Novak Djokovic displayed typical grace and sportsmanship in defeat. But Andy has firmly secured his place in Scottish sporting folklore. He is one of the greats of the game and his success today will inspire a new generation of tennis champions."

David Cameron welcomes newly-crowned Wimbledon champion Andy Murray to Number 10

Every picture tells a story, and on this historic occasion, every fan takes a picture

THE WINNERS

THE WIMBLEDON ROLL OF HONOUR

Year	Winner	Year	Winner	Year	Winner
1877	Spencer Gore	1923	Bill Johnston	1969	Rod Laver
1878	Frank Hadow	1924	Jean Borotra	1970	John Newcombe
1879	John Hartley	1925	René Lacoste	1971	John Newcombe
1880	John Hartley	1926	Jean Borotra	1972	Stan Smith
1881	William Renshaw	1927	Henri Cochet	1973	Jan Kodeš
1882	William Renshaw	1928	René Lacoste	1974	Jimmy Connors
1883	William Renshaw	1929	Henri Cochet	1975	Arthur Ashe
1884	William Renshaw	1930	Bill Tilden	1976	Björn Borg
1885	William Renshaw	1931	Sidney Wood	1977	Björn Borg
1886	William Renshaw	1932	Ellsworth Vines	1978	Björn Borg
1887	Herbert Lawford	1933	Jack Crawford	1979	Björn Borg
1888	Ernest Renshaw	1934	Fred Perry	1980	Björn Borg
1889	William Renshaw	1935	Fred Perry	1981	John McEnroe
1890	Willoughby Hamilton	1936	Fred Perry	1982	Jimmy Connors
1891	Wilfred Baddeley	1937	Don Budge	1983	John McEnroe
1892	Wilfred Baddeley	1938	Don Budge	1984	John McEnroe
1893	Joshua Pim	1939	Bobby Riggs	1985	Boris Becker
1894	Joshua Pim	1940	*NC (World War II)	1986	Boris Becker
1895	Wilfred Baddeley	1941	*NC (World War II)	1987	Pat Cash
1896	Harold Mahoney	1942	*NC (World War II)	1988	Stefan Edberg
1897	Reginald Doherty	1943	*NC (World War II)	1989	Boris Becker
1898	Reginald Doherty	1944	*NC (World War II)	1990	Stefan Edberg
1899	Reginald Doherty	1945	*NC (World War II)	1991	Michael Stich
1900	Reginald Doherty	1946	Yvon Petra	1992	Andre Agassi
1901	Arthur Gore	1947	Jack Kramer	1993	Pete Sampras
1902	Lawrence Doherty	1948	Bob Falkenburg	1994	Pete Sampras
1903	Lawrence Doherty	1949	Ted Schroeder	1995	Pete Sampras
1904	Lawrence Doherty	1950	Budge Patty	1996	Richard Krajicek
1905	Lawrence Doherty	1951	Dick Savitt	1997	Pete Sampras
1906	Lawrence Doherty	1952	Frank Sedgman	1998	Pete Sampras
1907	Norman Brookes	1953	Vic Seixas	1999	Pete Sampras
1908	Arthur Gore	1954	Jaroslav Drobný	2000	Pete Sampras
1909	Arthur Gore	1955	Tony Trabert	2001	Goran Ivanišević
1910	Anthony Wilding	1956	Lew Hoad	2002	Lleyton Hewitt
1911	Anthony Wilding	1957	Lew Hoad	2003	Roger Federer
1912	Anthony Wilding	1958	Ashley Cooper	2004	Roger Federer
1913	Anthony Wilding	1959	Alex Olmedo	2005	Roger Federer
1914	Norman Brookes	1960	Neale Fraser	2006	Roger Federer
1915	*NC (World War I)	1961	Rod Laver	2007	Roger Federer
1916	*NC (World War I)	1962	Rod Laver	2008	Rafael Nadal
1917	*NC (World War I)	1963	Chuck McKinley	2009	Roger Federer
1918	*NC (World War I)	1964	Roy Emerson	2010	Rafael Nadal
1919	Gerald Patterson	1965	Roy Emerson	2011	Novak Djokovic
1920	Bill Tilden	1966	Manolo Santana	2012	Roger Federer
1921	Bill Tilden	1967	John Newcombe	2013	Andy Murray
1922	Gerald Patterson	1968	Rod Laver		

*NC - No Competition